Journeys of Voices & Choices

by

Ernie Brill

Dedications

To my wife, Randy Ross
High school sweetheart, found years later.
Takes me from nervously something to beyond everything.

To the artist George Leys
My high school mate whose gifts enhance my life

To Dan Georgakas (1938 – 2021)
Cultural Pioneer, Urban Poet, Sharpest Critic
"I want you with me in the revolution, but you better tie your shoes!"

Published by Human Error Publishing

www.humanerrorpublishing.com
paul@humanerrorpublishing.com

Copyright © 2024
by
Ernie Brill

All Rights Reserved

ISBN: 978-1-948521-68-0

Cover Art George Leys

Table of Content

Brooklyn, Jews, Family

Work

Viet Nam

Middle East

Education

The Black Lives Matter Hybrid Haikus

Variations Towards Love and Peace

Brooklyn, Jews, Family

Cremation

My perpetual starvation bellows, burning,
Gaping open for more piles of humans.
Shove in more bodies! Feed my bottomless desire!
Yearning night and day I roar, devour
All the Jewish flesh crammed into me!

I crave blood by truckloads, trainloads FEED ME!
Bring communists, Jews, gays, gypsies, deviants,
All dissenters to my flaming abyss!
My conflagration crackles blood-red orange
With an unending hunger surging
To char, roast, broil and searing scorch them all!
I am the connoisseur of annihilation:

Let my churning smokestacks mark my power!
May the glowing sparks I belch torch the night!
Use the ashes and the billion bits of bone
To make new roads that shall last forever!

2020

Some wonder why I have not been dismantled.
Some ask I commemorate consciences' chasms.
Some shudder. A few grin, nod approval.
In their clenched hands my potential gathers.

My Mother's War Story

You young have no idea what it was like.
We lived for letters, for the slightest word.
I remember one night – I'll never forget it,
It was rough times, early in the forties,
We heard about your father on the radio.

His name was in the news, an article -
The storming of Kasserine Pass in Africa.
An article by a one Glen McFadden
Who turned out to be an A-One phony,
Describing a raging battle in Tunisia!!
Fighting Rommel, and that Rommel was tough.

They said your dad stormed the pass with a machine gun!
Such nonsense: he barely knew how to shoot!
But there we were: cold January, rationed heat,
And I didn't know where he was or how he was,
Or if he was dead or alive or what!

I didn't know what would happen to him
Or all of us. I was always worrying
If we could get to Europe soon enough
To save those in the concentration camps.

That evening I heard on the radio
The Germans had retaken Kasserine Pass.
It grew late, colder, I was miserable.
I wrapped the one blanket I had tighter
And tighter, like when I was a little girl.
I won't forget that night as long as I live

My Father's War Story

I had a fascinating job after the end,
Screening German prisoners of war here
To find who'd been antifascist. They didn't know
I spoke Yiddish and German fluently.

A horrid thing happened. I discovered
A thug posing as an anti-Nazi.
This monster tortured people in the camps,
And here he lectured on "democracy."

Four others were vicious SS vermin,
Planning their escape to South America
To meet other Nazi scum in Brazil
To re-start a new, improved Third Reich.

I couldn't believe it! I was beside myself!
I went right to the top; you should have seen me,
And exposed them. Those crooks! That filthy slime!
I said, "The only place you're going is six feet under!"

I couldn't believe my ears! But it worked out.
The dirty rotten bastards, I fixed them.

Mitosis

I was born in 1945:
We celebrated just being alive;
For who could calibrate the cost
Of the smoking cauldrons of the Holocaust?

Lately, I sense a strange impression
Of sources of my and my mom's depression.
Some swear it's genes; Science claims it's true.
I maintain other features factor too.

I read an essay in a magazine:
A therapist for many years has seen
Jews and others with a strangling sadness
That, on occasion, converts to madness.

She feels that many post-war mothers' wombs
Struggled with a stupefying doom.
I daydream, muse: did in her placenta
Another fetus of growing terror enter?

Of all who died by 1945
Thousands of skeletons were found alive
By Russian and American GIs
So stunned rumor claims the sights maimed their eyes.
Can I re-feel my mom's nine months with me,
She transfixed by newsreels tragedies,
Paralyzed by grim-skinned starving faces
Whose gummed spit seeded her inner spaces?
Did horror flourish in our blood-streams
With eerie nourishment beyond despair?'
Did minute fingers clutch and claw our dreams
Of the barely sensed malformed scrabbling there?
That, later, for me and my mother Bess
Became a subterranean process
Shrinks might dub PTSD regression
A stillborn-again source of our depression?

To my mind there's no ifs, buts, or maybes:
I was born with a complex choking twin
Tangled with a mangled sibling within:
A blood-red, half-dead bawling Holocaust baby.

Why I Panic When I'm Late

Maybe it's my heritage,
Echoing the centuries' deluge,
Announcing, "Quick! Time to leave
Before the Pharoah grabs us (Got the matzoh?)!"
"Run home to the ghetto before sundown eve
Or the ruffians or police will throttle ya!"
"Never go beyond the Pale
If you know what's good for you. Use your sense
Leave now or fall into the lethal veil
Of the Inquisition's malevolence."
I don't want to make a fuss,
But where is this train taking us?
If that's panic, what's left? When the world's deranged,
We can only live what we dare to change

"Aren't you going to Temple tonight?"

I write stories of Jewish triumph and conflict,
Showing our lives to the ignorant.
I wrap and unwrap my feelings uneasily.
I teach Eli Wiesel's Night to illuminate the day.
I go to Temple in my own way.

Great Moments in Baseball

A Scene in Slocum' s Bar the Night
Hank Aaron Broke Babe Ruth's Home Run Record
"Aaron's DONE it!" Peter bragged;
"DID it! BROKE it!" Stan, half-bagged:
"Balls just ain't the same these days,
Players don't make the same great plays,
Overall pitching quality's worse,"
Stan mumbled in his booze with a hissing curse.
"Come on, Hank's GREAT! Those whipping wrists!"
"Yeah, yeah," Stan muttered, drinking, pissed.
Al grinned, "Hell, Stan, records're made to be broken."
Stan scowled as Pete agreed, "Well-spoken."
"Henry Aaron, he ain't squat
Next to the Sultan of the Swat!
Ol' Babe'd point to where the ball would land
Then put that fucker in the stands!
Wush the god-dam GREATESHT, unnerstand?"
"Babe was GREAT, a legend true,
But, hell, fella, Hank's great too!
I think there's room for both, don't you?"
"Yeah," Al added, "What's bugging you?"
"Not a goddam thing, just talkin' sports."
"Seems more than that; Get it off your chest."
"Oh yeah? So you think you know wa'sh best?"
In the whiskied air in Slocum's place
Three men closed in, face to face.
"What's up, pardner?" Pete scratched his head
As Stan, reddening, sneered, "Drop dead!"
Tense arm tightening, gripping his liquor,
He blurted, "Goddam Aaron nigger!"

Singing In Brooklyn

We were singing on the benches We were singing in the parks
We were singing for our building We sang way past the dark
We were singing on the swings We were singing by the slides
Arms around each other we leaned in to harmonize
We were singing on the sidewalks We were singing next to cars
We were singing to the twilight We were singing to the stars
We were singing to our sweethearts not too late and not too soon
We slow danced with Nebulas wrapped our hearts around the moon

We were singing to the trees singing in the breezy night
We were singing to the world and for everything that's right
We were singing to the Lindy We were singing to the Stroll
The Cha-cha and the Philly We rocked and we rolled
We sang to streetlights the moon was quite surprised
We sang to mahjong tables flanked by fireflies
We were singing to the ice cream men, the delis, pizza places,
To the million games we played-handball, stickball, running bases

We sang to the Dodgers and to Jackie Robinson
We sang for challenges and we sang for fun
We were singing for our crushes We were singing for our loves
We sang on project rooftops to the Milky Way above
We sang to Coney Island and we sang to Brighton Beach
We sang to our dreams many thought beyond our reach
We sang in subways leaving the names of our girl friends
With markers, paint, spray cans, and multicolored pens
We were called depraved graffiti vandals yet we unfurled
Undergrounds firing fast fingers round the world

We sang for yesterday and looked forward to tomorrow
We sang for whatever we could con or steal or borrow
We harmonized our high notes with such high elation
We forgot to get off when we came up to our station
We were singing by the jukeboxes singing in the joints
From Sheepshead Bay to East New York,
Crown Heights, and Greenpoint;
From Downtown to Williamsburg Fort Green and Park Slope

A Daughter's Questions at Four

Can mountains dream?
Why do snakes shed their skin?
Can trees fall in love?
When can I fly?

The Meteor and the Daffodils

Bipolar, schizoid – call it what you will.
He'll bounce through flaming nights and storming days;
A meteor pats bees in daffodils

His family won't admit he's deeply ill.
Their desperate love deprives them of insight.
He once patted bees in daffodils.

Any offered love he tries to kill.
His strange hell only sees his private lights –
Bipolar, schizoid – call it what you will.

I cannot get my obsessive fill
Of his rambling blogs zigzagging through nights,
Recalling patted bees in daffodils

I cannot name the pouring pain that still
Mirrors rain in the mourning's wintry light –
Bipolar - schizoid – call it what you will.

All I now can do is wait until
He sets himself on fire, or sets himself right
Bipolar - schizoid – call it what you will.
He once caressed buzzing daffodils.

At Sea

When I heard you were drowning
I took out my heart
And made a red sailboat
Praying you'd grab rope
Clutch side barnacles
Hug hull
Grip anchor
Anything to save you
From roaring waves
And underneath a bottom
Plunging deeper
Than my treading heart
Wrestling storms
To bring you home

Work

Butcher

30 years
in the slaughterhouse
assembly line
30-55 cattle an hour
moving at an uninterrupted rate
hit over head with sledgehammer until
1950 then bullets used
skinned steer
pulling 200 pound hides
off each carcass
cleaned it
cut cow in two
carried away
buckets full of guts
pressure to get job done
at certain pace
strictly observed
breaks 15 min am 10 min pm
half hour lunch
optimum 400 a day
bosses worked over
them pushing

first chest pain 1975
condition not improving
1976 hospitalized 7X
final diagnosis congestive heart
failure resulting in expiration
flesh unto flesh (he was Catholic)
and there's more than one way
to skin a cat

Math Class

Figure at the minimum
1 steer every two minutes
30 steers an hour

48,000 pounds of hide each day
240,000 pounds of hide a week
12 million pounds of hides a year
2 weeks vacation

Working over 30 years
That's 360 million pounds of hide a year
One guy
Two hands

Intake

Elderly man
Silvery hair
Modest blue serge suit
Leans forward anxiously
Holds his left arm with care
He has severe arthritis
The Symphony told him
Consider retirement
At 61 he only knows
The violin
The Musician's Union referred him here
He wants to hear
Possibilities
and options
Of job retraining
He's willing to work
His handshake's gentle, full
Of fingers, like lonely iron
His smile's warm and waiting
Like the soft curious scrutiny
Of an unsure bluebird

Printer's Helper

Printer-proof reader daily exposure
To following substances:
Lampblack, paper dust, resins, benzenes.
Other ink fumes indigenous to field.
Talcum powders daily used to dry proofs
Poor ventilation constant condition,
Open pots of lead melting, paper dust
Constantly in air, stuck to clothing,
Continued resins presence raised dust amounts —
Everything covered with it –from machines
To employees to final product—
Everything having to do with the company

Current diagnosis: cancer, throat, left lung

Longshoreman

Art's work for thirty seven years involved
Working the docks of the Bay Area.
"My ships come in from all over the world.
You name the country, I unloaded it."
Some holds had asbestos dust so thick
Art couldn't see coworkers three feet away:
"We never got the gear guys get today –
Didn't happen 'til the late forties
And the Big Strike when the Union came.
Where'd I work? What did I work? Let's see now.
Pier Thirteen: cotton pants from Korea.
Pier Eight: Brazilian cowhides – Boy, they stank!
Pier Twenty was Australian wool
Pier Thirty-Nine: copper from the Congo.
Can't forget my favorite one: Pier 7
Jamison's whiskey crates from Ireland.
"I'll tell you what you can do for me, son,"
He wheezes, sucking his respirator,
"Far's the money goes, I'll get by.
Better if you get me some new lungs."

The Shapes of Minnie Evans

Her room's a white square
Her bed's a white rectangle
Her dialysis silver cylinders, loops
Her brown face a pained oval
Her smile a red semicircle
Round the circle of her poised family
Round the doctors' rounds outside the room, mum
Round were her buckets in endless hotels
Of cylindrical mops, deep square carts
Round the disinfecting bubbles in buckets,
Hexagonal the bubbles' carbon tetrachloride
(They showed her an organic chemistry book)
That formed and deformed her cancerous kidneys
Round is her body under the fresh sheets;
Round the dark red bottle under her bed
Yet what shape forms in the eyes of her son
Who stares at the 9 pm harvest moon?
What shape her daughter fluffing her pillows?
What shape her goodnight-to-her-grandchildren voice:
"Be good. You all come back and see me soon now. "

Ed

Sickly yellow cancer of the throat
He talks and rattles on pinched gritted teeth
Scrunched up in pain and undersized blue bedclothes
Don't treat me like a kid I know I'm going
They take my skin wha'd you say your name was
From all over my body Brill Brill Brill
I knew a guy named Brill my legs ass arms
He owned a used car lot in '32
And sewing it to my throat up in Revere
What a crook bastard I'm telling you
But it don't do no good nah not a damn
Or was it Charlestown he'd sell his mother
You're just a kid what do you know   for a nickel
I'm rich I own three houses   where's that nurse
Won 'em at the dog track   You Catholic kid?
Can always tell a good Irish boy   cocksucking nurse
Where's that pain pill   him and Joe Devaney
Got hot cars and change 'em   Billy Brill
Brother was a fighter   repainted them
He couldn't take a punch   twelve operations
They soaked me good them doctors did   but he could take a
dive
          Did they fix me   tell that nurse I'll have her canned
glass jaw
          You go to church? I don't   the cops got wise
Billy and Devaney   Katy's kid
Lot of good it did me   I won't leave here
Bought 'em off might as well try to fix the sun
One time down in Quincy   where's that damn nurse
They had this little racket going, see

On and on he croaks not so much to me
But to Death
As if Death is his publisher
And Ed's pushing hard
To get it all in on time

Breakfast

It's about time you came. I called and called,
Just like last night Nobody comes.
I'm left here to die Where's my juice?
Wait – this isn't the breakfast I ordered –
I ordered scrambled eggs and sausage.
This here's fried eggs and ham Oh, damn it all!
No, no, that's not my writing I should know.
Someone's falsified my menu. Figures.
Everyone's after my money Think I'm loaded.
What a joke! Have I got news for them!
How much did they pay you, sonny,
To bring me the fried eggs and ham, huh?
You think I was born yesterday?
A likely story I know it's getting cold
O K O K I'll try it OOPS! Oh dear! Sorry!
Can I help you clean it up? How clumsy of me!
Oh well, might as well get another tray.
Get it right this time: poached eggs and bacon
Two pieces of toast. Trim the crust.

Infected Leg

Hi there and the top of the morning to you
It's a beautiful day Saw the doctors
You'll never in your life guess what they told me
They won't be amputating after all
Scratch that order for the mahogany leg, pal
We knew it was a pipe dream anyway
Besides, the pocketbook's strictly plywood
I'll continue on antibiotics,
Wait and see if this odd swelling goes down,
Let them know when this awful smell goes away
They're wanting to talk with the wife when she comes in
I warned them not to be trying nothing funny
My Mary's faithful, and a tigress too
So you're stuck with me for a little while longer

Downsizing and God Bless You

Tissue is the issue
With Kleenex
Piled in a box Blow nose
Or hacking, spit,
Crumble,
Discard
For excessive cold,
If necessary, repeat
When the box empties,
Buy a new one
Check for discounts

Living Tissue II

We are grabbed, used
Snatched, dispatched,
Too beslimed for recycling
If only we could graduate
Become a handkerchief
Crouch in the pocket over
The area claiming
To be the heart

The Good Old 9 to 5

Understaffing infuriated us

Many were doing the work of two

With no new hiring

We petitioned the administration

My supervisor called me in

We want to do well   We're eating our hearts out

My supervisor gave me a napkin

Wipe your lips he said You're drooling

The Orderlies
(Essential Workers?)

How 'bout we go smoke a little bowlful?
We both deserve a little somethin', nope?
Damn! We both still smell God-awful.
I'm glad that's over with myself. Let's hope
He sleeps and don't wake up again all night
Or it's even money he'll unload again Right:
We rowing up Crap Creek, ya think?
No help –just you and me the whole damn watch.
Row, row, row your boat! Batten down the hatches!
Take the last; I'm good. What? Abandon ship?
Sure, laugh Quit NOW? You want a big fat lip?
I'm Captain Stench. And you're my First Mate Stink.
We save three hundred pounders best we can.
Overboard the Good Ship Bedpan; hell, we, HEROS, man

Patient Request

Look – I don't want him touching me.
It ain't that I'm prejudiced, believe me.
I'm always for live and let live;
You go your way and I go mine, you know?
I'd just prefer if you'd take care of me.
I feel more of what they call a rapport with you.
I'm sure it doesn't mean a rat's ass to him.
You understand me, you know what I mean?
Even though you're a little too quiet
To my way of thinking.   So, look, do what you can
To fix things up, ok? OK? Hey,
Buddy, are you deaf or something?

The Ballad of El Dorado Town

It started out a sleepy cattle town
with a waterhole in the middle of Main Street
until that fateful day when Arlen Brown
found a silver nugget at his feet

Chorus:
Morgan Mines and Silver brought progress to the town
money to burn, new schools to learn,
and the railroad coming 'round
the town shone brightly as we dug day and nightly
in beautiful El Dorado town

Sandy sold his farm, so did Mike and Zeke
Banker Dan says eleven farms were sold within the week
Bought by an Eastern man with a gold watch chain
Morgan from Chicago was his name

Oh they sank shafts so fast and struck up timbers too
Some folks wondered would it last and would it do
Asking Morgan, "Think them logs will hold?"
He nodded, dreaming past them, "Where there's silver, there's often
gold "

Chorus:
Morgan Mines and Silver brought progress to the town
money to burn, new schools to learn,
and the railroad coming 'round
the town shone brightly as we dug day and nightly
in beautiful El Dorado town

It happened quick like the flick of a candle wick
One twilight an explosion shook the depths;
Mine Seven timber's gave a hundred men a grave
Laying down beneath the shining silver

Women ran from doors and screamed from windows
Wondering which one was a widow,
Waiting for the cage with their man to rise
Their twilight hearts a-pouring from their eyes

Now Morgan gently spoke to the bereaved
"I'd give the world had these men been saved,"
Then he ordered up the coffins and the wreaths,
And placed a silver nugget on each grave

Chorus:
Morgan Mines and Silver brought progress to the town
Money to burn, new schools to learn and the railroad comin' round
The town shone brightly and we dug day and nightly
In beautiful El Dorado town

The Fat of The Land

We've waited decades for the trickle down
Some of us wear well-worn neck braces
From tilting our parched mouths up to the sky
They say there is a fair play headquarters
Neither side negotiates with spirits
When hard facts of contract time come around

Once with leaders we stormed the restaurant
Now we negotiate sizes of spoons
There's chanting by the dishwashers;
You tuck your face in fat white cloth napkins,
No longer needing to roll up your sleeves
Veterans know- uh oh - crumb time again
You can't hear the screaming in the kitchen
Because you've forgotten how to turn up the heat

The Work Poets
(And Now for a Brief Non-Commercial)

I do not understand
Why are they not in most anthologies?

Sterling A. Brown, John Beecher, Meridel Le Sueur,
Eugene Rolfe, Muriel Rukeyser, Franklin Marshall Davis,
Kenneth Patchen, Kenneth Fearing, Thomas McGrath,
Naomi Replansky, Tillie Olsen, Melvin Tolson, Gwendolyn Brooks

And many new ones — Pedro Pietri, Janice Mirikitani,
BH Fairchild, Benjamin Saenz,
Phillip Levine, Marge Piercy, Frances Chung,
And the newer - Simon Ortiz, Paola Corsa, Peter Oresick,
Patricia Smith

What did they do to achieve such invisibility?

Viet Nam

Children's Hour in Vietnam
(Parts I – IV)

I. NONSTOP BIRTH CERTIFICATE
World Airways swears
This orphan's genuine
They shot the fake father at the airport,
And shoved the phony mother into the sea;
150 bucks to Friends of the Children
Gives this kid a home for its newfound freedom

II. POSITIVE ID
Another surefire orphan
Her father a suspected sympathizer
Expired in a Pleiku tiger cage
And a Red Cross aide saw her mother
Pass away in a strategic hamlet
Trying to bite through the barbed wire

III. REPORT FROM THE EMBASSY
I haven't seen such wholesale tragedy
Since I flew for the Flying Tigers in Korea
I haven't seen such wholesale tragedy
Since I rowed Batista's relatives out of Cuba
Pack my darkest shades
I hear that Kuwait sun's a bitch

IV. AND NOW FOR SOME BREAKING NEWS
TV commentator goofs
Runs a censored clip
In liberated Hue whole families
Greet Viet Cong with flowers
Lines of teenagers happy as little kids
Grip rifles pointed straight at Saigon

After Battle

You claimed we were mighty arrows,
Sighting freedom's bullseyes to save democracy,
Even if innocents perished in war's perils

But why did so many archers die?
Why do so many broken bows litter the land?
Why so many warriors stumbling down side streets?
Why so many one-legged ghosts?

By the Lawn Chairs in the Backyard

As far as the media goes,
Consider me an unusual Vietnam vet:
I've never been to the V. A.
I have a good job, and a family:
Wife, daughter, son; we own our house.
I drink socially, never in bars .
I've never been homeless, never jailed
I have no nightmares or P T S D.

I'll never tell what happened over there
Because of my faith   I don't want God's ears to bleed

The Woman's Road

This highway is called The Woman's Road.
I will tell you why we call it that.
After Viet Nam's wars, women who fight
Long years in forties, fifties, and sixties,
Many helping to build Ho Chin Minh Trail,
Come back. They've grown old. Hard to get married.
Hard to find husband. Hard to find boyfriend.
They set up stalls, sell food and drinks to drivers
Who maybe give them a happy little something
(Because in Viet Nam it's much better you have
A child to help you and take care of you).
Then the women go into the forest,
Find village where no one knows them, start new life.
Later, they come back along the road,
Sell food and drinks to the drivers.
Their child cares for them and their ancestors.

This is why we call this The Woman's Road.

[Note: In 2013, I spent two weeks in Viet Nam, with my wife, our daughter, Shivani, and her fiancé, David. A very knowledgeable tour guide told us this story.]

Viet Nam Haikus

Pho

Each breakfast millions
Of hands stir steaming soup bowls
Warming Viet Nam

By the Ocean

The ocean's fullness.
Empties out my soul,
Leaving only windy sun.

A breeze stirs the heat.
Welcoming the sea,
Women laugh and splash.

Blue serenity
Soothes tight weariness.
What is the world this moment?

If you pass my name,
Leave me your laughter
To wink in the hereafter

Water whispers, "Be humble.
You're a visitor.
We're here forever."

Ha Long Bay

Sea mountain tower
Huge caves fit whole schools
Above pink fishing houseboats.

Mountain Fairy Meets Dragon
Of the sea. They love.
Their son guards the land.

If there is trouble
The sun rises from the waves
To save the people

Our tourist boat paddles past
Famed "Kissing Chickens"
Two sea stacks lean, smooch

Middle East

After The Bomb

I went out for pizza
And ate all my blood.
I went to buy shoes,
And saw my foot fly through the air.
Hold me, mother
For the last time, hold me.

Jesus in the Shadows

You chased the moneylenders from the temple
Your transformations turned the world upside down
How would you act now as wounded
Armed Palestinians take refuge
Steps from the shadows of your refugee first breath?

Would you again thunder from the mount
Turn the other cheek, perform miracles
In the nearby hospital parking lot
Come help bury bodies decomposing
Since war's curtailed the morgue's electrical power?

Will you, change-maker, re-tissue the dead
So the bereaved can wholly mourn
Past bulldozers gouging expedient pits like
Mass graves where Nazis stacked machine-gunned Jews?

The Occupation of Palestine

The sky is occupied
The trees are occupied
The thyme is occupied
The sea is halted at a checkpoint
God's Hands are UP in the air
At gunpoint

RUSH!

Be ambulance Be siren
Be swirling red lights
SCREAM YOUR THROAT OPEN

Mother Earth:

Move over, Abraham   Excuse me, Hamid
We need room in this expanding graveyard
Under the earth our singing bones grow
Knowing no border no stops no country
If you're not sure this claim is in order
If you're not sure this claim is true
Feel the voices and music flowing through the ground
And let the dead report back to you

Towards Healing Passovers

We wanted a home I understand: centuries
Of smashed doors, unparalleled wanderings.

Yet what's the limit when we arrive home
At the price of others' evictions
Without creating new exiled ones?

Is it only Elijah, and not Mahmoud
For whom we keep the door open
And offer a plate?

Israel Negotiates with PLO Leader Arafat

Surround his inner sanctum
With a cordon of tanks and snipers
Cut off his electricity   Blockade his food

Declare him enemy   Demand
He come to the table for talk
After you pull out the chairs
And set them on fire

Elegy for an Unknown Human Falling
(9/11/2001)

I see you leap from the flaming tower.
You jack-knife, freeze in midair by camera,
Tucked, seeming so disciplined, calmly poised
As you plunge, what beats through your heart and brain?

Do you remember your mother making breakfast,
Or your child crying out in the night?
Do you recall triumphs – first breath held underwater,
Or, simply, calm Sunday afternoon strolls?

Do sudden fleets of seagulls cushion you,
Winging you to a warm haven?
Or do you behold Buddha, Allah, Jesus
Whose wide embraces spirit you to safety
Before looming concrete arrives and air ends.

I wish tensed thousands, gathering, linked arms
To form impromptu human trampolines
To bounce you past death. And I wish
Angel firefighters aimed cloud-hoses
Whose waterfalls could drown conflagrations.

I wish myself and a million others
Could lift the rubble, wipe away the soot,
Cradle your crushed body and, bending, breathe
Over your lips, and bring you back to life

Where Were Your Flags?

Where were you when they bombed Hanoi's children's hospital?
Where were you when Death Squads raped nuns in El Salvador
And murdered priests?
Where were you when from Chile to Indonesia
Embassies and "advisors" engineered overthrows,
Democratic leaders disappeared, dropped from planes?
Where were your tears then?
Where were your flags?

Can You?
(Looking at a Photo in the News)

Feel the frost on four Afghani children
Who, crouching in the coming winter, cradle bowls
White (whiter than bleached bones), empty, cold,
In waiting calm. They wait to be fed.
Staring with a cautious optimism ahead
That coats a mountain hunger we've not climbed,
Deepening all four bowls like valleys bombed –
White craters on the world's stripped negatives
Where the near obliterated scratch to live.
Perhaps the four white bowls bear resemblance
To satellite dishes illuminating soon
Communications via the full moon,
Rebounding light to awaken numbed consciences.
When our snows soon start to descend, my friend,
Ask where those bowls begin, and where they end.

Education

Early Childhood Education

They arrive brimming with wonder,
Entering like young thunder.
Years later, why do so moping many
Complain of constant boredom, listlessly
Fret and shrug around the room, sigh-searching
For the memory of inner lightning?

The End of the Faculty Meeting

For schools competing in a global world
Critical thinking's absolutely key
To help stay in context on the same page
And not waste time on questions off topic
That could be researched in other venues.

By lining up all our ducks in a row
We establish measurable components
To show us where we need more improvement
And areas where we exhibit strength,
Understanding that, while change takes time,
We must raise the levels of expectations.

I know there's only a few minutes left,
But does anyone have any concerns? If not,
Thank you for all that you do. You're dismissed.

"A.I."
(Artistic Inspiration)

Our imaginations offer treasures
Your calculations cannot understand
We bring global gifts you cannot measure

Artists world-wide know the trembling pleasure
Of journeys sparked by hint or hunch unplanned
Unknown outcomes are imagination's treasures

Some think art's a hobby, dabbling leisure
And not a note in eternity's band
Whose music surpasses its own measures

Throughout history society censures
We who break old lines for zig-zagging lands
Summoning imagination's treasures

The timid and the tedious prefer
To pressure artists, keep us close at hand,
Squeeze us into square holes they can measure

Today most honest artists will concur
Soaring past charts, graphs, and vital brochures,
We often concoct, create new treasures
That light worlds beyond what you can measure

To The School Bullies

How many of you brave ones does it take

To slam Henry Li into a locker,

Throw Lara Rosa's books down the hallway,

Push Leshayne Bontemps down the staircase?

Five? A starting basketball team?

Six? A hockey squad?

Nine? A team to play ball?

Eleven -All lines working together?

As Henry Li winces,

As tight-faced Lara gathers kicked belongings,

As Leshayne, fists clenched, immediately jumps up,

How many of you brave ones know in no time -

With a sneer's turn, a mood's pivot, inside out,

It might be you.

Black History Month

O K Kids, I'll need your help today
To take down the Black Inventor Posters
And put them away for next year's class.
Please go through your folders and choose
Your writings and pictures of Dr. King
And other special people we've studied
To take home and show your parents.
What's that, Janie? Why did Dr King have to die?
Now that is a terrific question, Janie!
And I'm sure you're fourth grade teacher next year
Will be happy to explore that but for now,
We need to get ready for our new Math Unit -
A neat one on Subtraction! You're gonna love it!"

The Further Adventures of Tarzan

TARZAN KING OF THE APES LORD OF THE JUNGLE
GREAT WHITE GOD OF UNENDING KNOWHOW
TAMER OF SAVAGES ARYAN BRINGER
OF SENSE AND CIVILIZATION TO AFRICA!
BOYSCOUT FOR IMPERIALISM
SUPERMAN IN A G – STRING!
tarzan, he got old, man, jane got tired of doing all the housework
kicked his ass out the tree took herself a sugar-daddy lover
archeologist jewel thief doubling as a priest (episcopalian)
and tripling as a peace corps ngo prexy with a hotline to high places
boy was away at the time in counterinsurgency school
so tarzan alone tried to sweep through his jungle
grabbed a vine, missed, dove, cracked his tailbone,
screamed for his faithful elephant zazoo who rumbled by silently,
having just signed a no-cut contract with big apple circus;
his pet ape cheetah hung close relieving himself,
mulling the possibilities of usurping
tarzan's cocaine empire

Meanwhile, back at the treehouse
The local population rebelled burning
The treehouse
Tarzan's Purple Heart
His Silver Star
His Green Beret
His stocks and bonds in French and Swiss cartels
His complete works of Joseph Conrad and Rudyard Kipling
Did Tarzan quit? Never, mired in mud,
He trilled his famous yell to his loyal lions
Who eagerly sped to the scene (having not eaten for days)
Jumped joyfully on him, pulling, tugging, licking
As hyenas gathered, scratching patiently

The Black Lives Matter Hybrid Haikus

Black Lives Matters Hybrid Haikus I

Harlem

Reaching for ID
Immigrant Diallo dies
Forty-three police shoot

Henry Dumas, author of The Echo Tree and Other Stories
Subway, NYC

He descends subway
Three transit cops shove and shout
He never comes out

Ms. Eleanor Bumpus, Queens, NY

Eleanor screams, shrieks,
Struggles hard with officers,
Then shuts up for good

Subway Platform Michael Stewart, NYC

Cops stop, search actor
He reads them his rights
He had a very strong voice

And In Brooklyn

Arrest: suspicion
Haitian man tortured by cops,
Raped with a night stick

Scrap Scrape, George Baskett, San Francisco

Police car scrapes truck in alley
Driver and cops shout
Cops draw, take him out
In front of son, three

Laquan McDonald of Chicago's New Math

He's sixteen years old
Cops shoot sixteen times
Measure, solve for unequal

Jordan Davis, Jacksonville, Florida

Watch your IPOD, son
Wrong tune, dude shoots you
You'll never listen again

Trayvon Martin, Miami, Florida

I got my skittles,
Gonna see my girl
Hey, man, don't point that at me

Freddie Gray, Baltimore, Maryland

Cops grabbed, gave him a long ride;
Returned D O A
What happened inside?

Michael Brown, Ferguson, Missouri

Corpse on ground all night
Cops won't let his folks touch him
His hands were in the air

Walter Scott, Columbia, South Carolina

Shot four times in back
Cops deny the fact
Bystander filmed the act

Eric Garner, Staten Island, NY

Sells illegal cigs,
He's neighborhood known
He's asthmatic Cops attack

He cries, "I can't breathe!"
Struggles to be free
Can't gasp past strangling chokeholds

NY PD bans
Court rules against the murdered
Blue perps go free

Tamir Price, Cleveland, Ohio

I like playing here!
BANG! GOTCHA! BANG! BANG!
Hi, Officer I was just -

Alton Spurling, Baton Rouge, Louisiana

He hawks used CDS
Cops arrive in parking lot
No more sales Ever

Sandra Bland, Waller County, Texas

Stopped for not signaling
Insists on fairness hotly
Found in cell hanging

Lavish Diamond, four-year-old stepdaughter of Philando Castille, Falcon Heights, Minnesota

Dad point-blank dying
Mother clenched crying
"It's ok Mama; I'm here "

Oscar Grant, Oakland, California

Can't make it tonight, baby
At Fruitvale Station
This cop shot me dead

Ahmaud Arbery, Harwood, Georgia

Goes on daily jog
Stalking vigilante guns
Cancel his last run

Daunte Wright, Minneapolis, Minnesota

Black man stopped Cop shrieks: 'TASER!"
Shoots three times: HE'S DEAD!
She serves sixteen months

Amir Locke, Minneapolis, Minnesota

No-knocks bust door kill
In nine seconds this sleeping
Wrong innocent man

Patrick Lyoya, Grand Rapids, South Dakota

Stopped for minor infraction
Beaten to the ground
Shot dead point blank

Breonna Taylor, Louisville, Kentucky

Cops storm the wrong place;
Friend defends; police shoot eight rounds
Pummel sleeping EMT

George Floyd, Minneapolis, Minnesota

Leaning on his neck – "CAN'T BREATHE"
Cops present disgraced
Mugging thugs murder the law

Rayshawn Brooks, Sequoia, Georgia

Asleep: Wendy's Lot
Cops wake, make him walk drunk line
Shove They fight He's dead

Elijah McQuade, Aurora, Colorado

Shy musician, mental woes
Police overmedicate
No more clarinet

Alex Toledo, Chicago, Illinois

Chicago Cops torpedo
Alex Toledo
Gun? Was on the ground

Black Lives Matter Jazz Hybrid Haikus II

Louis Armstrong

Orphan lifts his horn
The moon somersaults
The saints come marching in

Lil Armstrong

Lil plays piano
Rocking with her left
Writing next set with her right

Duke Ellington

When Duke's mother died
He filled her church with
Thousands of yellow flowers

Coleman Hawkins

He played his heart, inside out
Blood flew everywhere, earth soared
Even when he wept, Christ he swung,
Even stars kept time, tapping

Billie Holiday

Billie brought the ooo oooo ooooo
What a little moonlight can do
Breathless meanings mean to me
Her starlight-in-reverse trail terrifies:
The night, sailing backwards, plunges
Into a sea of roaring gardenias

Assorted Hybrid Haikus III

Haikus flow gently
Missing most massacres
The world screams in pain

Immigrant

We clean your toilets,
Your lawns, your kids too
When we're gone, what will you do?

Savages

La Migra rips families
Crams kids in cages
Who marches for them?

Memories of Great People:

Malcolm X

Bonfire eyes blazed
Devoured whole libraries;
Read the riot act

Harriet

Eyes grip the North Star
Heart grips will and gun
Leads hundreds to first freedoms

Cave Canem Praise Poem

CITIZENS   IN THE MECCA   Service Porch
Maverick Kaleidoscope OLIO   Autobiography of a Jukebox
Muscular Music   Leadbelly Jellyroll   Life According to Motown
Shoulda Been   Jimmy Savanna Hip   Logic   Up Jumped the Boogie
Rhyme Scheme
Incendiary Art Wild Hundreds   City Ecologues   Drawn in a Box
Fearsome   Maverick   Life on Mars   Leaving for Saturn   Hoops
Venus Hottentot Quantum Lyrics   Testament
At the End of the Alphabet   Magnolia   Rise   Bestiary   Ordinary
Beast   Kingdom   Swag   Skin Inc.   There Are More Beautiful
Things Than Beyonce   The Goddess of Gumbo   The Gospel of
Barbecue Mess and Mess   Don't Let Me Be Lonely   Play Dead
Bring the Shovel Down   Little Edges   Don't Bury the Dead
Magical Negro
Natural Birth   Freedom Ventures   Antebellum   Homeplace
Craving Radiance   Mystic Fury   Head Split   Close   Big Town
Big Talk Whereas   Madwoman   Thrall   Southside Rain
Captivity   Buck Studies   Brutal Imagination   Digest   Totems
Golden Shovels   To See The Earth Before The End of The
World   Blood Dazzle

Praise Song for African Literature

Things Fall Apart   No Longer at Ease
We Killed Mangy Dog   The Real Life of Domingo Xavier
The Time of The Butcherbird   In The Fog At Season's End
The Smoke that Thunders   Weep No More Child
On Trial for My Country   Man of the People
To Every Earth Its Blood   Emergency   The Arrow of God
The River Between   Tribal Scars
The Old Man and the Medal   Secret Lives
Houseboy   The Wretched of the Earth
My Life in the Bush of Ghosts   Hammer Blows
The Purple Hibiscus   Half a Yellow Sun
Black Docker   Stone Country   From a Crooked Rib
Hopes and Impediments   The Beautiful Ones Are Not Yet Born
The Healers   Petals of Blood
Poor Christ of Bomba   Devil on the Cross
The Thing You Wear Around Your Neck   Sweet and Sour Milk
Hammer Blows   The Last of The Empire
Return to My Native Land   God's Bits of Wood

Why African American Literature Is More Than Window Dressing

Damballah   The Chosen Place the Timeless People
HUE AND CRY!
AND THEN WE HEARD THE THUNDER! RUN MAN RUN!
TRAGIC MAGIC   CONJURES   FEARSOME   AVALANCHE
ANOTHER COUNTRY PRIMITIVE   REAL COOL KILLERS
CRAZY TO KILL BUCK STUDIES
Push Humid Pitch Close to Death Hog Butcher Blood Dazzle
Skin Inc.   Elbow Room We Can't Breathe The Heat's On
Captivity Narrows World of Nothing Middle Passage
Flagellants Trouble the Waters Many Thousands Gone
Known to Evil   Fear Itself   Tempest Tales
Fragments of the Ark Ark of Bones Amistad   Salvage the Bones
Freelance Pallbearers   Walking Through Darkness   Catacombs
The Long Fall   Yesterday will make you cry

Many Rivers to Cross   Sing Unburied   Sing the Song Yet Sung
Undertaker's Daughter   Don't Call Us Dead
Bring the Shovel Down   Brutal Imagination
Venus Hottentot   Solid Gold   Holding Company
The Underground Railroad Tradition They Shall Run
Flight to Canada

The National Guard   OLIO   Their Eyes Were Watching God
Testimony   The Known World   Of Mules and Men
Southern Road Cane Spunk
Native Son   Lost in the City   Knock on Any Door   Nobody
Knows My Name   The Outsider   No Name in the Street
Rites of Passage Body In Question

Don't Erase Me Lawd Today Passing Quicksand Just Above
My Head   Lonely Crusade Rise   Youngblood Black Thunder
Blood On the Forge

Always Outnumbered Always Outgunned   All I Did Was Shoot
My Man Hold 'Em 'Til It Hurts   If He Hollers Let Him Go
Good Morning Revolution   Wild Hundreds   We Are the Ones
We Have Been Waiting For   Future Land   The Future Has a Past

Blue Light   Blues People   Stomping the Blues   The Weary Blues
Mojo The Blues   Blueschild Baby   The Bluest Eye   Her Blue Body
Everything I Know
Song I Want Witness   Nightsong   Song of Solomon   Clicksong
Hum Darktown Follies
Victim of the Latest Dance Craze   Autobiography of a Jukebox
God's Trombones   Gideon's Trumpets   Tambourines of Glory
A Different Drummer Banjo Cranial Guitars
Play Ebony Play Ivory Fingering the Keys   Leadbelly

Tell Me How Long This Train's Been Gone   Just Above My Head
Two Cities   Philadelphia Fever   A Rage in Harlem   Cotton
Comes to Harlem   Harlem Gallery   Home to Harlem   Iron City
Lot   Come Back Sweetwater Conjure Woman

Possessing the Secret of Joy in the Temple of My Familiar   Mama
You Can't Keep a Good Woman Down   Clotilde   Our Nig
Dessa Rose   Corrigadora Iola   Muriel   The Bondswoman
Cora Unashamed   Catherine Carmier   Sula   Coal
The Autobiography of Miss Jane Pittman Faith and the Good Thing
Two-Headed Woman   Quilting   Blessing All Boats
Rainbow Jordan God Bless the Child   Price of a Child
Tar Baby   Uncle Tom's Children   Montgomery's Children
Aunt Hagar's Children   These Bones Are Not My Child
This Child's Gonna Live!   Sons of Light and Darkness
Craving Radiance   Incendiary Art   Hoops Maverick   Jelly Roll

A Man Aint Nothin But a Man   The Invisible Man   Man in My
Basement   Going to Meet the Man   The Man Who Cried I Am
In My Father's House   A Gathering of Old Men   Eight Men
 Captain Blackman   All Night Visitors   Dem   Reckless Eyeballing
Junior Bachelor Society   Cotillion Bang Groove and Jive Around
Mumbo Jumbo   A Lesson Before Dying   Healing Debridement

Ballads of Remembrance   In the Mecca   No Hiding Place   'Sippi
Bombingham   The Fire Next Time   Sent For You Yesterday
The Spook Who Sat By The Door   Black Water Rising   The Negro
Caravan   The New Black   Love's Instrument   Tuff   Home Girls
and Hand Grenades Semi-Automatic Neon Vernacular   Black Fire
Black Woman   Push   Push Comes To Shove   The Fire This Time

Trouble Is What I Do

Images of Kin   The Marrow of Tradition   Honorable Amendments
Parable of the Sower   Kindred   Dr. King's Refrigerator and Other
Bedtime Stories   History Is Your Own Heartbeat   The Seabirds Are
Still Alive The Good Lord Bird   Paradise The Dreamer The Echo Tree
The Long Dream   Gorilla My Love   Mercy   Home
The Oxherder's Tale   Conjure   Jubilee   Dancers on the Shore
For My People   Dancing in the Streets   Black Voices
Go Tell It on the Mountain   Beloved

Variations Towards Love and Peace

The Chestnut Man

The chestnut man shuffles in the wind,
Remembering (perhaps) with Christmas shivers
Clear spells ago that gave him dreamless sleep.
His silent peace and hot chestnuts warm us;
We taste autumn's heart, crisply hear New Year's
Approach. Trying to pluck secrets, we laugh,
And sniff the wondering air that rings, so hushed,
A very simple bell: the voice of snow,
Bright welcomer, bringing hints of embrace.
Shy incredible sky wells up with light,
And falls, fresh, soft, supple – such a kiss –
Touches with trembling grace the chestnut man,
Patiently tending his fire, smiling at those
Who guess he's near the Magi and mingle with his gift

Momentary Builders at the Seashore

Remember building with gleeful devotion
Moated sandcastles at the edge of the ocean?
Crouching, we shaped and conjured fantasies
Transformed towards art ascending afternoons
'Til striding surf threatened our creations Soon,
We met the rushing challenge and the thrill:
Tide surged. Our work swayed, yet stayed, but still
We knew our desperate hands could not outpace
The instinct of the ocean to erase.
We scrambled, yelling on our muddy knees,
Viewed ocean's waves as friendly adversaries
Who lent time to imagine and pretend
Then showed in telling twilight how things end:
In evanescence, vanished boundaries.

To Z from Kansas City

"Deer weep in your eyes "
You knew well. Your aching gaze
Caressed pink gazelles

Sudden

I wish my memory worked worse.
I wouldn't remember your touch,
Recall your laugh,
Behold your face.
Hearing your name
Wouldn't crush my breath.

Ode to the Hunchback of Notre Dame

I am Quasimodo.
You are Esmeralda.
I have rung my last bell,
I'm leaving the church alive.

I'll haunt the terrible pews,
Disturb religious hypocrisy,
Take my twisted face
Toward new streets and new scorn,

Knowing in my backbone's horror-show
Only the gargoyles will miss me.

Polar

My fingers freeze
Touching our cracking Antarctica.
Icebergs fill eyes.
The playful penguin's dead.

All seals left before dawn.
On a dissolving floe
A polar bear bellows
In the disintegrating tumbling snow.

April Twilight

We gave each other roses,
But now it's time to pull up roots.
We gave each other roses
But now it's time to pull up roots .

Turn the earth over. Seek
New gardens. Seek new shoots.

If your heart like mine,
Feels torn and hot,
If your eyes, like burnt flowers,
Sting, petal by petal,
Remember –
Spring's sharp for us

Turn the earth over.
I'm turning over the earth
Going deep
And, like the blade of a shovel,
The sharp crunch
Echoes in the flesh.

Regret

The doors of your laughter swung wide open
But I couldn't reach the torn tears in the back rooms
The flowers you left inside me bloom every year
Then fade

Maybe I didn't water them enough

Sparkling Haiku
(For RR)

You arrive so alive
The full moon's astonished
A glow claims the world

In the Deli of Life

Wandering from counter to counter
Looking here and there
What did I encounter?
Past the pickles, potato salads, herring in sour cream
Suddenly I saw you as if in a dream
The counterman leaned over, "What will it be?"
I didn't even have to point; I knew what was for me
I saw you
Standing hands on hips
Oh yes I knew
What I wanted for my lips
So forget the hot pastrami
Skip the brisket too
Baby all I want
Is to share a bite with you ooo oooo oooo

Hold the ketchup
Keep the mustard
Never mind the sauerkraut
I relish a special order
I can have here or eat out

In the Deli of Life
I found my special wish
Don't want no cream soda
Don't need no knish
In the Deli of Life
I lost my appetite
But I found what could fill me
From the morning to the night
It was YOU
In the Deli of L I I I IFE

My Beloved in the New Millennium

Before I met and smelled your hair again
I was disappearing behind shut doors,
Half-living in a crumpled house of anxious air
On a bed of dust with wasting dreams
With only two young flowers and glowing shreds
Of remaining roots to keep me alive.
Bold, laughing, you opened the windows
To meadows of joy's maroons and delight's blue breezes
To new moonlight
Filled with orange trees,
Bringing to our mutual table
The soup of love and the bread of justice.
Now under your mangos,
Tongues, and oceanic compassion
I bring you anemones and singing
To share the simmering naivete named hope
That the juices and wild ferment of our lives
Will outlast the barrens and all desert storms.

The Seven Seas Blues
(for RR)

I love you baby
More than every wave in every sea
Yes I love you baby
More than every wave in every sea
The ways you move me baby
Make me captain of the world
Oh don't you see

We don't need a compass
We find new ways to navigate
We don't need a compass
We find new ways to navigate
I'll sail with you to anywhere
Just bring me to your dock and starting gate

It's almost as if the moon, baby,
Was made for only you and me
It's almost as if the moon
Was only made for you and me
The moon is Heaven's trunk
And the stars all the leaves in Heaven's tree

Take my captain's hat, baby
And wear it on your head
Take my captain's hat, baby
And wear it on your head
But you can take it off, baby
Whenever it's time for bed

The Blossoming
(A Wedding Poem for RR)

Wandering for forty lost years
In desert ablaze dying of thirst
I met a flower I'd known before
A flower I'd held before
And knew the radiance was no mirage

Again, the petals took my breath away
Again, I knew to my shaking roots
The springing ground was again beautiful
We are each other's oasis
Here figs arrive, oranges sing
Olive trees glow, palms flourish
Each line, each song, each leaf, each branch, each fruit,
And we two make up the jazzy caravan
Journeying as one joyous passenger

A Newer Never-Ending Story

(For Terry Collins, Jerry Varnardo, Margaret Leahy, and all the Good
Troublemakers of the 1968-69 successful student strike against racism at
San Francisco State College)

We all pass, yet our best never die.
They permeate the earth, refresh the air.
I don't know where they go, but let me try.

Many friends are going, and that's no lie.
Some go by fire, some laid to earth with care.
Some dawdle – difficult to say goodbye.

Concentrate in quietude. Try
To hear them singing. Do you dare
Ask if they can do new things, like fly.

Margaret, Terry, Jerry will look straight in your eye,
Chuckle, "You have no idea what's up, up here!
We have fifteen new demands. Want to see?"

What matters way much more is memory.
They remain a supersonic tonic here
We still can see, hear, feel them, share our glee.

Steadfast and still so close, there still will be
Magic moments – come touch their face or hair.
Oh yes, we pass but our best never die.
They rally with us, so why say goodbye?

Mt. St. Helens

(for Meridel Le Sueur)

By Dan Georgakas and Ernie Brill, at The Foolkiller Center for
Alternative Learning, Kansas City, Missouri, June 1980

She did more than complain
She did more than decry
She did more than lament
She did more than demonstrate
She did more than protest
And above all
She did more than rebel

From the depths of her violated womb
Upon the throats of the gluttons
She hissed ash

She buried them

Thanks, Acknowledgements

To my teachers, lions among mice....
Naomi Tiger, Jacob Wolis, Peggy Hillsgrove, Howard Shivera, Jim Fike,
Steven Sparacio, Elmer Ruhnke, Herbert Kauffman, Richard Weisman,
Eric Solomon, Michael Krasny

To the scintillating poets who inspire and guide me....
Theodore Roethke, William Butler Yeats, Sterling A. Brown, Pedro Pietri,
Gwendolyn Brooks, Mahmoud Darwish, Pablo Neruda, Tadeusz Roze-
wicz, Frances Chung, Muriel Rukeyser, Hyesoon Kim.

Special thanks to poetry percolators over the years....
Jim Willems, Amy Jackson, Rob Frede Kenter, Jan Clausen, Robert
Roth, the Toward Revolutionary Art folks (John Levin, John Curl,
Fernando Barreiro, Eli Shul, Dan Cassidy, Leslie Simon, Aisha
Kassahoun), Paul Yamazaki, Frances Chung, Steve Cannon, Quincy
Troupe, Chris Gonzalez, Tongo Eisen-Martin, Tom Clark (aka Tommy
Twilite)

To the publishers of my poetry....

Museum of Poetry	"Crematorium"
Raven's Perch	"My Mother's War Story"
Poetica Review	"Mitosis"
Gideon's Trumpet	"My Mother," "End Game," "Haiku for RR," "For Z in KC"
The Greenfield Recorder	"She Patted Bees in Daffodils"
KONCH	"Why I Panic When I'm Late," "Back-packing with My One-Year-Old"
Silkworm	"Singing in Brooklyn," "Ed"
Harbor Publications	"Butcher," "Math Class," "Breakfast," "Infected Leg" in *Going for Coffee: An Anthology About Work* (1981)
Red Wheelbarrow Press	"Longshore"
Anti-Heroin Chic	"Longshore"
Ice Flow Press	"Housing Officer," "Intake," "Printer's Helper," "The Shapes of Minnie Evans," "Beautiful El Dorado Town," "Work Poets"

	"The Fat Of The Land"
Oddball Magazine	"The Orderlies"
UMass Online Poetry:	"Downsizing"
John Brown Press	"Children's Hour in Vietnam, Parts 1-4," "City Kids"
Against Achilles	"After the Battle"
Forbes Library Community Posting and Reading	"The Bomb"
Anthology for Peace in the Ukraine	"The Bomb"
Lunaria	"Towards Better Passovers"
Active Muse	"Jesus in the Shadows"
Daily Hampshire Gazette	"Elegy for a Human Falling"
Toward Revolutionary Art	"Jury Duty," "The Further Adventures of Tarzan"
Radical Teacher	"Early Childhood Education," "Black History Month"
FlowerSong Press	Black Lives Matter Hybrid Haikus (18 poems) in Good Cop Bad Cop (2021), ed. Edward Vidaurre & Vincent Cooper

Ernie Brill grew up in a lively Brooklyn project of freelance storytellers. Brill's pioneering fiction about hospital workers, I Looked Over Jordan and Other Stories (Boston: South End Press, 1980), was optioned by Ossie Davis' and Ruby Dee's Public Television Series "With Ruby and Ossie". Ms. Dee performed Brill's "Crazy Hattie Enters the Ice Age" to critical acclaim.).

Brill earned an MA in English from San Francisco State University and won a $4000 fiction grant from NEW YORK STATE COUNCIL OF THE ARTS.

He was the fiction editor for TRA (Towards Revolutionary Art Magazine) from 1972 -1979, and for Z magazine from 1986-1996. Brill has spent a fair portion of his adult life working with alternative small presses and championing them, including Curbstone, Conditions, Firebrand, Thunder's Mouth, YBird, West End,Cineaste Film Magazine, Isthmus, and others.

He's published widely (River Styx, Other Voices, Ice Floe Press (Toronto), Dash, Atherton Review, Silver Apples (Ireland) Prentiss- Hall, (Ontario) and others. Favorite authors includ Virginia Woolf, Richard Wright, Mahmoud Darwish, Hyesoon Kim, Sterling A. Brown, Gwendolyn Brooks, and Damon Runyon.

"Ernie Brill's Journeys of Voices and Choices is timely in that it matters. It matters that we still have a voice. It matters. It matters that we still have the will to protest, to stand up and sit down in defiance and solidarity with all that is still held with the gaze of humanity. It matters that I read this book. It saves me and every so often on a seemingly quiet Saturday afternoon, it still saves me. It matters. It really matters."

Truong Tran, The Book of the Other and Placing the Accent

"Ernie Brill brings a thoughtful and insightful vision born of experiences and depths of emotion to this personal and political poetry. A long-time passionate reader and teacher of literature as well as a fighter for social justice, his work conveys a wide range of portraits from a rich inner world."

Michael Krasny, Professor of English Literature, Emeritus,
San Francisco State University

"Ernie Brill is a legit legend with a long history of walking the walk. His poems explore themes of work and justice while always keeping in mind the beat of the people. I am proud to call him my friend and fellow traveler.

Tom Clark, aka Tommy Twilite, Florence Poetry Society

"I'm amazed at the 'End Game' about your mother, and the poem about African novels. I doubt anyone's ever done a poem that way."

Jim Willems, poet and publisher of *Isthmus*, the first press to
publish the poems of Janice Mirikitani

Made in the USA
Middletown, DE
02 June 2024